Self-Editing for Indie Authors

21 Quick and Easy Tips for Better Writing, Positive Reviews and More Sales

Michelle Lowery

Edited by John Lowery

Cover Design by Fiona Jayde Media
fionajaydemedia.com

Formatted by Polgarus Studio
polgarusstudio.com

The author has made every effort to provide accurate website addresses at the time of publication, but does not assume responsibility for changes that occur after publication. In addition, the author does not have any control over, nor assume any responsibility for, third-party websites or their content.

Printed in the United States of America

For more information, please contact:
michellelowery.com

ISBN: 978-0-9977812-0-5

For John.

My husband, my best friend, my editor.

Contents

PART THREE

PART FOUR

PART ONE

INDIE AUTHORS AND THE BUSINESS OF PUBLISHING

Why I Wrote This Book

Being a published novelist is a dream I've had since I was a kid, so I set out to be an indie author to write and publish fiction. I have a handful of short story ideas floating around in my head, and a few bigger ideas that will eventually become novels. Some of them are started, and in various stages of completion. Now it's just a matter of putting butt in chair and getting them done.

So why the heck am I starting my indie author career with a non-fiction, how-to book on editing?

Because while I do believe writing—and even editing—have foundations in talent, they're also skills that can be learned and improved over time. I've been working on my writing and editing skills for more than 25 years now.

But I'm also an entrepreneur—**and so are you**.

I co-founded a Web copywriting and editing agency in the summer of 2013 after the digital marketing agency my business partner and I worked for went under. Prior to that, I'd worked in the digital marketing and SEO industry since 2008. And now I'm back to writing and editing on a freelance basis.

So for several years now, I've not only been writing and editing content, but advising clients on how best to create and use content for marketing, brand-building, and to increase their bottom lines.

One of the things I've advocated since the beginning is the need for high-quality content because, without that, you don't get the visible brand and strong sales.

When I began pursuing my own writing in earnest, I realized indie authors are also entrepreneurs. Their success also depends greatly on the quality of their work. And like entrepreneurs, they either do everything—including editing—because that's all their starting budget allows, or because they're true do-it-yourselfers.

And then I knew I had to write this book.

Indie Authors: Entrepreneurs of the Publishing Industry

While they don't get up and go to a workplace every day, have a boss, or receive benefits, authors in the traditional publishing model are almost like employees of the publishers who distribute their books.

Authors have to be accepted by a publisher who likes their work, much like being hired after an interview. They have deadlines to meet, editors whose changes they have to accept in order for the book to move forward, and then they receive a percentage of their book sales—a small percentage, because the publisher has to cover overhead, maintain a profit margin, and please shareholders.

The ability to self-publish has not only largely removed agents and publishing houses from the equation, it's allowed many writers to take their work and careers into their own hands, and create the lives they want.

It's given writers freedom.

Starting my own business wasn't only about continuing to generate income after losing my traditional job. It was about being in control and doing things the way I thought they should be done.

I wouldn't lose my business due to the mistakes made by the business owners for whom I had worked. I wouldn't be forced to work with clients from hell who made my workdays miserable. I could make my own choices and build something to be proud of.

And that's what you're doing as an indie author.

Sure, it's about making money. We've all gotta eat, right? And a lot of indie authors have the goal of quitting their day jobs to be full-time writers.

But it's also about writing what you want, not necessarily what's popular in the eyes of a big publishing house. It's about retaining ownership of your work and having control over when you publish—once a month, if you want to, rather than having to wait a year or more for your turn to come around.

It's about choosing the *want to* over the *have to*.

And that's the strongest bond between entrepreneurs and indie authors.

You're Running a Business

When you take any form of art and put a price on it, you turn that art into a commodity. You're no longer writing, painting, sculpting, or whatever just for fun, or as a hobby you do in your free time. You're now running a business.

No business exists without customers. As an indie author, you have access to a large and varied customer base.

They're called *readers*.

You may write for the love of writing, or because you're compelled to do so, or because you recognize the income potential. But if you expect readers to hand over their hard-earned money for something you wrote, it needs to be a worthwhile expense for them.

It doesn't matter whether your book costs $.99 or $9.99. When someone shells out cash, they expect to get something in return, preferably something good.

If you're not editing your writing before you publish—or having a professional edit for you—you're doing your readers—your *customers*—a disservice. As a business, it's incumbent upon you to create the best product possible for your customers. Don't you expect the same from the authors whose books you like to read, or from any business where you spend your money?

You're More Than Just a Writer

Entrepreneurs wear a lot of hats, some fancier than others. When they first start their businesses, often on shoestring budgets, they take on a lot of tasks simply because they can't afford to outsource them or hire staff to do them—yet.

Indie authors run into some of the same challenges. We've established that if you're selling your writing, you're running a business. That means there's bookkeeping to be done. And tax preparation. There's advertising and PR, as well as numerous forms of marketing—social media, email, content, and search. Those are just the business tasks.

Then there's the community and platform building. These tasks can be fun, but also quite time consuming.

As for your writing itself, it's not simply a matter of putting some words down in a document, and *voilà*—instant payment! If only it *were* that simple!

Once the writing is done, there's editing and proofing, formatting and uploading. There may be more formatting and paginating if you're releasing both digital and print books. You also need cover art, and maybe you'll run contests or other promotions.

My point is, as a writer and indie author—particularly if you're just starting out—you may find yourself doing more than writing, whether by necessity or choice.

Self-Editing vs. Professional Editing

Now, before anyone gets offended and says, "Hey! I self-edit, but that doesn't mean I'm not a professional!" I know. And I agree.

But in trying to draw a distinction between writers who edit their own work and editors for hire, it's quicker and easier to say "professional editor" than "editor for hire," or "external editor" (which sounds weird), or "editor you pay to edit your writing." So I'm going to stick with "professional editor," and we'll know I mean all of the above, OK?

Let's take a look at both options.

Self-Editing: Necessity, Preference, and Honesty

Why do so many indie authors self-edit?

- They're starting out and can't afford a professional editor.
- They're good at editing and feel more comfortable doing it themselves than handing their work over to someone else.
- They have an entrepreneurial DIY attitude, and like to be in control of the entire process.

- They *can* afford a professional editor, but they're confident in their editing skills and would rather put their money toward other expenses like cover art.
- Tons of other personal reasons unique to each writer who self-edits.

No matter what your reason is, the key is to be honest with yourself—are you actually improving your work by editing it yourself? Or could it be better if you sought outside help?

You may be a fantastic storyteller, but a not-so-great editor, and that's OK. The important thing is to recognize that's the case and address it appropriately so what you publish is of the best quality possible.

If you fall into the first category—you're not the best editor, but you don't have the budget for a professional editor—you still have options.

Barter. If you're not great at editing, what *are* you good at? Maybe you're an excellent book cover artist. Is there a writer/editor who could edit your work in exchange for a cover or two?

Learn. Editing, like writing, is a skill that can be learned. Sure, it requires some talent, and sometimes, it's instinct—knowing the flow isn't quite right, or having a knack for arranging words and sentences in more powerful and interesting ways. But it's also knowing grammar, spelling, punctuation, vocabulary, and the mechanics of writing. Look for books and resources (hey, like this one!) that will help you become a better editor, which will, in turn, help you become a better writer.

Seek feedback. Find beta readers who will give you honest feedback about your work. Family and friends may be willing to help, but they may also not be completely honest because they don't want to hurt your feelings. Look for beta readers who will give unbiased opinions, and who are familiar with your genre. It's not the same as an actual edit, but having a reader point out areas that consistently require improvement can lead you to the specific writing and editing tactics you need to learn in order to produce better work.

Don't give up. Do the best you can for now with one or more of these suggestions. Keep writing and publishing until you get to the point where you've either learned enough to be a confident self-editor, or can hire a professional editor. Only you can judge if and when either of those things happens.

Professional Editing: Convenience, Perspective, and Risk

Why do many indie authors go the professional editing route?

- They're excellent storytellers, but not the best editors.
- They love to write and hate to edit.
- They can afford to hire a good editor.
- They prefer an outside perspective on their writing.
- They would rather spend time writing more books or marketing their existing books than editing their unfinished ones.
- Tons of other personal reasons unique to each writer who seeks professional editing.

Again, all excellent reasons to seek professional editing. But let's explore one in particular—hiring not just any editor, but a **good** editor.

How to Hire a Good Editor

As writers run the gamut from outstanding, to good, to mediocre, to "it's time to choose another career," you'll find editors who've hung out a shingle, but don't know the difference between past tense and the subjunctive mood, or why it's "between you and me" and not "between you and I."

It pains me to read stories about indie authors being taken by "editors" who charged hundreds of dollars and either left the work worse than they found it, or skated by with nothing more than a few comma corrections.

Hiring an editor is like hiring any other service provider—due diligence is required. Some things to look for:

Do they have a portfolio? If it's not readily available on or through their website, ask to see it. What kind of writing and what genres have they edited?

Do they have testimonials, recommendations, or references on their website? If not, can they provide them to you directly?

What's their payment policy? It's standard to ask for 50 percent up front, and the balance upon completion of the project. If they ask for the full amount up front, do they guarantee satisfaction and/or have any kind of refund policy if you're unhappy?

Do they have a blog or any other writing? Read it. What does it look like? How does it sound? If you find errors or they're unable to construct sentences well, chances are they're also unable to edit well. Anyone selling themselves as an editor should have impeccable content on their site—that's their primary form of advertising. Would you let a stylist cut your hair if their hair looked like it had been cut with a weed whacker? I mean, unless that's the look you're going for.

What's their email communication like? The above also applies here. Can they communicate clearly? Is their correspondence free of errors?

Do they communicate with you in a timely manner? This is subjective, but you'll know what you feel comfortable with. If it takes them too long to respond to your emails, you may wonder whether they'll be able to meet editing deadlines.

Do they understand the need for preserving your voice? Editing should enhance and improve your writing—not change its style or the way it sounds.

You'll notice I didn't mention a degree or formal education of any kind. If that's important to you, and you believe a degree in English, Creative Writing, Journalism, or a similar subject is an indication of editing knowledge, ability, and prowess, you can add it to the list of things you look for in an editor.

But before you discount someone without a degree, consider all the other factors. How many authors have degrees in English or Literature? Not all of them, that's for sure, but it doesn't mean they can't write well. And there's a lot to be said for experience.

You may want to weigh education against experience. Would you prefer an editor who received their degree in English in the last year and hasn't held more than one job yet, or an editor without a degree who's been on the job for a decade, and has a solid work history and great testimonials?

I'm not advocating one over the other. I'm saying you have to choose what you think is best and what you're comfortable with.

Even if you find someone who seems to pass all of the above with flying colors, there's still a chance the editor you hire won't be as good as they say they are, or as good as you want them to be. You may not have good chemistry with them. They may not appreciate your writing or your genre.

The point is, if you hire one editor and have a less-than-ideal or even flat-out bad experience, don't give up and assume all editors are full of crap and a waste of money. As it takes time to find the hairstylist who makes you look like a supermodel, it may take a little time to find the editor who takes your good work and helps you make it outstanding.

Combining Self-Editing and Professional Editing

I'm both a writer and an editor. I self-edit because I actually enjoy it, and because it enables me to polish my work to the point where I'm proud and confident to share it publicly. I also self-edit because—I'll be honest with you—I'm persnickety.

I'm pretty sure most other editors aren't going to catch or be as conscious of the little details I look for, or that they won't be able to fully preserve my voice and style. Translation: Yes, I'm a control freak about my writing.

Now, that said, once I've edited my work to my satisfaction, I do hand it over to another editor, usually my husband, or a close friend who also self publishes, or both. They're both excellent editors, and they may provide me with more in-depth feedback than just adding a comma here or correcting a typo there, although they'll do that for me, too.

Some say it's a myth, but I believe the longer you've worked on a piece, and the more times you've read it, the less likely you are to see the typos and other little errors that may jump out at someone seeing your work for the first time.

I know because it happens to me fairly often. I know what I *meant* to write, so my brain plays a little trick on me and tells me, "Yup, that's what it says, all right!" This is why I seek at least one round of editing, or at least proofing, after I've edited.

I'm always grateful for their input—but I don't always incorporate it into my work. I maintain the final say on what stays, goes, or changes. You can always do that, too.

Seven Benefits You'll Get
From This Book

Like any business owner, you want to please your customers. But why? What's in it for you? Why should you care whether your readers are happy or not?

Because without customers, you won't sell anything. Period. Keeping your readers happy is a big part of your path to success as a published indie author, and this book will help you provide your readers with a better experience.

The three main benefits of this book are right in the subtitle: better writing, positive reviews, and more sales. One leads to the next, which leads to the next. But you'll get much more out of it than that. This book will provide you with not just three, but *seven* benefits:

More Effective Editing

If you're a self-editor, maybe you're already really good at it, and producing technically excellent books. If so, good for you! But we can all use a refresher from time to time. Or maybe you'll see a couple of things here you hadn't considered.

The tips in this book will make your editing more effective, meaning you'll miss fewer errors and stumbling blocks (I'll explain what I mean by that a little later), and end up with a cleaner, more polished manuscript.

Better Writing

When you go through your manuscript and edit out all the errors and fluff, it's also a learning experience. With each round of edits, you'll identify any bad habits you may have, which will make you more aware of them—and less likely to repeat them—when you're writing.

Each subsequent manuscript will be better than the last, which will also make your editing go more quickly and smoothly. It's a continuous win!

Positive Reviews

You know the most important feature of your book is its quality. But how is that quality conveyed to new readers who may not be as quick to take a chance on your work?

The answer is reviews.

When the quality of your writing is poor, you're more likely to get poor reviews, or at least, not get as many good reviews as you could otherwise. And the fewer good reviews you have, the fewer sales you're likely to make.

While you don't want a solid block of five-star, glowing reviews, which would look fake and like you might've bought them, you do want positive reviews. Even a two- or three-star review that mentions positive aspects of your work is preferable to a one-star review that is nothing but a complaint about finding too many spelling and grammatical errors.

And positive reviews lead to…

More Sales

This is a basic business concept. The better a product is, the more in-demand it is. Equally as important, the better and more in-demand a product is, the more you can charge for it. I don't mean you should bilk your customers if you get popular. I'm talking about value here.

If you release an unedited (or poorly edited) book, it may be reflected in the reviews that detail all the bad spelling and grammatical errors your readers find. And if that happens, how will you be able to charge an amount that will net you a good percentage? How will you build that into a living wage, and grow into a more comfortable one? How will you be able to charge *anything* with a clear conscience?

Your readers and reviewers will call you out on that faster than you can say "dangling participle," and you'll be forced to either drop your price and lose money, or go back, edit, then rerelease the work, and hope the existing negative reviews haven't ruined your book's chances of success.

Do it right from the beginning. Write well, edit well, get good reviews, make more sales.

Save Money Now

This is especially important if you're just starting out. Maybe you're still working full-time at a traditional job, writing before and after work, and during your lunch hour, and maybe even sneaking in a paragraph or two during work hours. You likely fall into one of two camps: You haven't published yet, or you've published, but haven't yet made enough money to hire an editor, let alone quit your day job.

Self-editing will allow you to release better work and save money on editing until you have a few titles under your belt and a few royalty checks in the bank, and are in a position to hire a professional editor, if you decide to pursue outside help.

Or, if you're good at editing, you enjoy it, and are a staunch do-it-yourselfer, you can consistently save money by self-editing. This can open up more budget for all the other things you need to run your business: covers, formatting help, giveaways, paid ads and other marketing, bookkeeping, and author assistant services, to name just a few possibilities.

Save Money Later

Even if you plan to hire a professional editor, you may still want to edit your first draft yourself at least once. This will not only allow you to make tweaks to your story or ensure accuracy of information, it will help you send a cleaner manuscript to your editor.

Some editors charge by the word or by the page, while others charge by the hour. If your manuscript's in pretty good shape when you send it on, that means less work your editor has to do, which can translate to money saved for you.

It can also mean you get your final draft back from your editor sooner, and get it published more quickly.

Know a Good Editor When You See One

The more you know about editing, the more easily you'll be able to recognize what a professional editor does—or doesn't do—to your manuscript. It's difficult to judge someone's work when you're not familiar enough with what they do, or what counts as quality work.

Should you fall in with a less-than-stellar editor, you'll be able to recognize that more quickly, and move on to find another, better editor. And when you do find that wonder-worker editor you're seeking, you'll know it. You'll also know you're getting your money's worth, and that you need to hang on to that editor with both hands.

A Note About Style, Dialogue, and Authenticity

English is a language full of nearly as many exceptions as rules. Spelling is a constant, but while some grammatical rules are hard and fast, others are subject to style and the preference of the writer or editor.

Fewer vs. *less* is a clear choice. Not as clear is *more than* vs. *over*. You'll have to make some choices depending on what you prefer, or what you think sounds better or more correct. The key is—and I can't stress this enough—**be consistent**.

If you write, "The warehouse contained more than 5,000 books," then stick with "more than" in similar structures throughout your writing. If, later on, you switch to "He encountered over 15 people in the gym," you may be creating a stumbling block for your readers.

As a quick aside, I also believe that people learn from the things they read, and unfortunately, they don't always learn correctly. When thousands of people see an ad on TV or in a magazine that contains a misspelled word or incorrect punctuation, they may assume that error is actually correct, and perpetuate it through their own writing. After all, a professional edited that magazine or that commercial, right? And they know best, right? So why wouldn't it be correct?

This is something I keep in mind when writing and editing. I want to make sure I'm not perpetuating errors by making my own completely avoidable ones.

Dialogue is a whole other issue.

The way your characters speak will depend on a lot of things—where they're from, their level of education (if that's a relevant and stated quality), and the time period and location in which your story's set, to name just a few factors. One or more of these could mean your character doesn't always use correct grammar, or that their accent causes them to pronounce words differently.

Depending on those factors, will it sound authentic if, for example, your character says *ain't* instead of *isn't*? Again, whatever dialogue patterns and quirks you choose for your characters, it's about consistency. Make sure your character doesn't start out with a certain way of speaking, and then inexplicably lose it halfway through the book.

How far you take dialogue quirks will be up to you. Just don't let a character with a penchant for bad grammar leak into the rest of your writing.

What This Book Isn't

This book is not meant to replace the services of a professional editor, should you decide that's your preference.

Also, this is definitely not a grammar book. We will delve into a little bit of grammar because I don't think you can talk about editing and *not* talk about grammar. But this is by no means any kind of textbook or thorough examination of the English language.

Finally, it's not a full-on course on editing. With as many ways as there are to write, it only follows that there are just as many, if not more, ways to edit. Style plays a big role in writing, and dialogue sometimes calls for bending the rules. Your editing will have to accommodate those features unique to your work.

What This Book Is

Put simply, this book contains 21 ways to make your editing more effective, thereby making your writing better. You'll also find editing method suggestions, as well as editing and writing resources.

As an editor, I run across several common mistakes a lot of writers make. They're actually small errors, but when made over and over, they affect the overall quality of your writing.

A few of the issues I'll discuss may not be outright errors. They're what I call *stumbling blocks*—little oddities that make readers pause to figure out what the author meant, or go back and reread sentences to understand them, both of which are burdensome to readers

Have you ever gotten to the end of a book and wondered how you arrived there? You were so engrossed in the story, you were blinded to words and pages. *That's* the experience you want to create for your readers.

The last thing you want to do is take your readers out of your work. You want them fully immersed in the world you've created for them. They should forget they're reading a story or a book, and be fully engaged through both your words and their imaginations.

Putting a stumbling block in front of your reader ruins that experience. Making them work to understand what you're saying makes reading, well, *work* instead of fun. It's your job to make the journey as smooth as possible for your readers, and keep them coming back for more.

Yes, it's about telling a good story. But all those little mistakes and stumbling blocks get in the way of the story. No one's paying attention to the story when they're counting typos or reading poorly constructed sentences over and over again. For indie authors, good writing and editing are tantamount to good customer service.

How to Use This Book

One of the best compliments I can receive is when a writer tells me my edits helped them improve not only the piece I edited for them, but their writing in general. I've always felt that rather than just taking the proverbial red pen and marking up a document, good editing includes explanations of the *why*, and in some cases, examples to illustrate those reasons.

To make putting these editing tips into practice a little easier on those of you who aren't ardent word nerds like me, I've done the same thing here. I'm providing a short reason, a full explanation and at least one example for each tip.

You can skim this book, read the short reasons, and take my word for it if you like, or you can read the full explanations and understand the *why*. Yeah, the full explanations may get a little heavy on the grammar and pedantry, but I think retention is improved by understanding the reason behind something. Plus, I think grammar is fun, although I know I'm usually in the minority there.

But I also think we learn something more thoroughly when we understand *why* it is the way it is. That understanding leads to retention, which leads to better writing, which leads to less need for editing. It's a constantly improving cycle.

And if you don't have to do as much editing, you can get your book to market much more quickly, start bringing in those royalties, and dive right into that next book.

It's my sincere hope that you find this book helpful in some way. Whether it's knowing you're not alone in tackling all the writing and business tasks, or finally being able to choose the right pronoun for your prepositions, I truly hope you take away something useful.

Why You May See Some Repetition

Because I've structured this book to be easily skimmed, you may not read it from beginning to end, and you may not even read all of it. That's OK. But if you *do* read all of it, you may see a few things repeated.

I've done this intentionally so those who do jump around and maybe skip a tip or two will still get the same explanations where they're applicable. So if you're a front-to-back reader, thanks for understanding and not emailing to scold me for repeating myself. I promise, it's still a quick read.

So let's get to it!

PART TWO

21 QUICK AND EASY SELF-EDITING TIPS

1. Get Rid of *That*

I'm starting with this one because I'm pretty sure I see it more often than any other stumbling block. While overusing *that* can usually be overlooked in speaking, it really stands out in writing. If done too often, it can look, at best, like padding for word count, or at worst, like a lack of articulation and the inability to explain something without using *that* as a crutch.

The Short Reason

The majority of words and phrases can stand alone without adding *that* as a bridge between clauses.

The Full Explanation

It's difficult to explain this one without an example to illustrate it. Here's what I'm talking about:

> The reason that so many people tend to use *that* in their writing is either that it's a bad habit, or that they're unsure that they can properly explain an idea that they have without it.

Now let's take out the extraneous instances of *that*:

The reason so many people tend to use *that* in their writing is either it's a bad habit, or they're unsure they can properly explain an idea they have without it.

Put it Into Practice

The best way to avoid the evil *that* is to read your work out loud. If you find yourself repeating *that* over and over, imagine how it's going to sound to your readers. It quickly becomes tedious, and it's unnecessary, as you can see by the second example with the word removed.

What I tell writers when I'm editing their work is, if you can take *that* out and the sentence still makes sense, **do it**.

2. People are People...so Why Would You Use *That*?

Here's another instance when you shouldn't use *that*—when referring to people.

The Short Reason

That is for things; *who* is for people.

The Full Explanation

That and *who* are relative pronouns. They are often used to signal the beginning of an adjective clause, a phrase that will describe the thing or person you're talking about. For example:

> The book that won the Pulitzer Prize was written by a first-time author.

The adjective clause *that won the Pulitzer Prize* describes which book you're talking about.

> Judy is a teacher who specializes in biology and chemistry.

The adjective clause *who specializes in biology and chemistry* tells what kind of teacher Judy is, and because she's a person, *who* is the correct relative pronoun.

Put it Into Practice

This is pretty easy, and the short reason pretty much covers it. Just remember, people aren't things!

3. That vs. Which

We've talked about how to cut down the use of *that* when it's not necessary, and when to replace *that* with *who*. Now let's talk about when to use *that* or *which*.

The Short Reason

That indicates a clause essential to the meaning of the sentence, while a clause constructed with *which* can be removed without changing the meaning of the sentence.

The Full Explanation

This is about the difference between *restrictive* and *nonrestrictive* clauses.

A restrictive clause does exactly what its name suggests—it restricts another part of the sentence in which it appears. Essentially, the restrictive clause cannot be removed without changing the sentence's meaning, or simply causing the sentence not to make sense at all.

A nonrestrictive clause puts no such restriction on the rest of the sentence. You can remove the nonrestrictive clause, and the meaning of the sentence will remain intact.

Restrictive clauses begin with *that*.

Nonrestrictive clauses begin with *which*.

Put it Into Practice

So how do you choose between *that* and *which*? Like this:

> The book that won the Pulitzer Prize was written by a first-time author.

You're not talking about just any book here. You're talking about *the book that won the Pulitzer Prize*. Without that restrictive clause, the meaning of the sentence changes, and you could be talking about any book written by a first-time author.

The clause is essential to the sentence, and therefore uses *that*. You'll also notice this instance of *that* cannot be removed without making the sentence sound odd.

Now let's change it around a bit to illustrate *which*:

> The book, which was written by a first-time author, won the Pulitzer Prize.

If you remove the nonrestrictive clause *which was written by a first-time author*, you are left with the book you're talking about—the one that won the Pulitzer Prize. The nonrestrictive clause is simply providing a little more detail, but it's not necessary, and taking it out doesn't change the meaning of the sentence.

Let's look at a couple more examples:

I don't like blankets that are itchy.

I don't like wool blankets, which can be itchy.

In the first example, if you remove the restrictive clause *that are itchy*, you're saying you don't like blankets in general. That's not true, is it? Even if it is true, this should still help you remember whether to use *that* or *which*.

In the second example, the nonrestrictive clause *which can be itchy* is providing a bit more information about why you don't like wool blankets, but it's not really necessary. You can remove the clause, and the sentence will still make perfect sense.

Now that *that's* out of the way, let's move on to more tips!

4. Me, Myself and I

Not only do I see a lot of people misuse *myself* in writing, I hear people do it when they speak, too. For example:

> Myself and Alex are going to the conference next month.

> If you have any questions, please call Anna or myself.

The Short Reason

Myself is not the right pronoun to use in those examples. It should be *I* and *me*, respectively.

The Full Explanation

Let's get this straight right now—*myself* doesn't go anywhere or do anything. That's because *myself* cannot be the subject of a sentence.

Like verbs, pronouns take different forms depending on the situation. The two basic forms are subjective and objective. Subjective forms are *I, we, he, she,* and *you.* This means those pronouns can act as the subject of a sentence, and perform action.

Objective forms are *me, us, him, her,* and *you* again. They can be either direct or indirect objects of a sentence, and receive action.

Myself is a reflexive pronoun, which means you would only use it when you are performing an action on yourself, such as talking to yourself.

Put it Into Practice

The easiest way to know which pronoun is correct? Take the other person out of the sentence. So in the first example:

> Myself and Alex are going to the conference next month.

if you remove Alex, you have:

> Myself is going to the conference next month.

Would you ever really say that? No, of course not. You'd say:

> I am going to the conference next month.

It doesn't matter how many other people are going to the conference with you, *I* is still the correct pronoun because you're one of the subjects of the sentence who is performing the action of *going*.

The same applies in the second example:

> If you have any questions, please call Anna or myself.

Take Anna out, and you're left with:

> If you have any questions, please call myself.

Again, would you say this? Do you ever say to someone "Call myself."? No, you say "Call me." This is because *me* is the objective form of the pronoun, and is receiving the action of *call.*

It doesn't matter how many other words or how many other people you add to the sentence, *me* remains the correct pronoun.

By the way, when you do have other people in the sentence, they should always come first:

> Alex and I are going to the conference.

> If you have any questions, please call Anna or me.

5. Verb—That's What's Happenin'!

This makes little difference when speaking, but makes all the difference in writing. I often see verbs and prepositions put together to form single verbs. Two common examples are *setup* and *login*. Both are incorrect.

The Short Reason

Setup and *login* are nouns, not verbs.

The Full Explanation

Both words are created by combining a verb (*set* and *log*) with a preposition (*up* and *in*). It's important to remember which words are actually the verbs, and you'll see why when you try to use the progressive aspect of the verb.

The progressive aspect indicates action that is ongoing or in progress, and usually ends in *-ing*.

Put it Into Practice

If you're in the process of putting your home office together, what are you doing?

setting up your home office

You use the progressive aspect of *set* to show action that is taking place and is not yet complete. If *setup* were the verb, then the progressive aspect would be:

> setupping your home office

Looks ridiculous, right? And it is. Think about it for a minute, and you'll understand why it looks ridiculous to write, "I'm going to setup my home office this weekend." Instead, to use these words as verbs and a noun, it should be, respectively:

> I'm going to set up my home office this weekend.

> You have a really nice setup for your home office.

Same goes for *login*. Are you loginning, or logging in? Right.

A few more of these to watch out for:

> work out / workout
>
> work up / workup
>
> break out / breakout
>
> break up / breakup
>
> pick up / pickup
>
> lay out / layout

lay off / layoff

knock out / knockout

kick off / kickoff

hang out / hangout

Now, as English is wont to do, it's going to throw a little wrench into the works—the hyphen. When should you use set-up and log-in?

Answer: When you need them to be adjectives. Good thing we're going to talk about that in the next section!

6. Compound Adjectives

Now that we have *setup* and *set up* straight, what about *set-up*? You've seen that too, right?

Usually, hyphenating two (or more) words like this creates a compound adjective. But not every compound adjective will be hyphenated. Also, some of them will be one word, while still others will remain two or more separate words.

English isn't one of the most difficult second languages to learn for nothing, you know.

The Short Reason

When you combine two or more words to be one adjective, hyphenate them—usually. You may want to read the full explanation for this one.

The Full Explanation

When you create an adjective by joining two or more words, you need a way to indicate that they're both describing the same noun, and doing so in a way that is different from the way the noun might be described by those words individually.

You also need to ensure the sentence correctly conveys your desired meaning.

To accomplish both of these goals, use a hyphen.

However, when the first word in that compound adjective is an adverb that ends in –ly, do not use a hyphen.

These rules apply when your compound adjective **precedes** the noun it's describing.

When it **follows** the noun, do not hyphenate—usually.

And finally, there are some instances where two words can be put together to form a one-word adjective. Again, this structure will occur when the adjective precedes the noun, not when it follows.

We're going to need several examples here. Let's go one by one.

Put it Into Practice

Compound adjectives that **require hyphens**:

I actually just used one: *one-word adjective.* I was referring to an adjective that is composed of only one word. This is clearly indicated by the hyphen. A few more examples:

set-up instructions

eight-hour workday

16-year-old boy

ten-story building

500-page book

high-quality writing

end-of-year sale

heart-healthy meal

twenty-first-century technology

well-rounded person

You'll notice the last example begins with an adverb. However, because *well* does not end in –ly—and because it can also be an adjective (and a noun, and a verb, for that matter)—you must use a hyphen.

How can the meaning of a sentence be affected by compound adjectives that are not hyphenated when they should be? Like this:

I saw a man eating tiger in the jungle.

Did you actually see a man who was eating a tiger in the jungle? If not, then you saw a *man-eating tiger*.

Compound adjectives that **do not require hyphens**:

fully functional android

aptly named book

Compound adjectives that **follow nouns but still require hyphens**:

The suspect was a 16-year-old.

The meal was bland because it was heart-healthy.

Compound adjectives that **follow nouns and do not require hyphens**:

His writing is high quality.

She's well respected.

Now let's mix it up a bit:

This technology is from the twenty-first century.

You'll notice *twenty-first* is still hyphenated because it's describing *century*. However, although *century* is technically also describing the technology, it stands alone. It's actually the object of the preposition *from*.

Compound adjectives that can become **one-word adjectives without a hyphen**:

The best example for this is the one I see most often—*everyday*.

I wear jeans and T-shirts every day.

This indicates something you do on a daily basis, on each individual day.

Jeans and T-shirts are my everyday clothes.

In this instance, *every* and *day* are put together to create one adjective to describe a type of clothing.

An easy way to remember this is to think about another expression we often use:

I wear jeans every single day.

The fact that you can separate *every* and *day* in this manner to describe when an action is performed should remind you not to use *everyday* for this type of specification.

7. Acronyms, Initialisms, and Their Articles

Acronyms and initialisms are both types of abbreviations. Which article you use with either—*a* or *an*—will depend on whether you're using an acronym or initialism, and how it's spelled or structured.

The Short Reason

Like regular words, acronyms and initialisms take either *a* or *an* depending on whether the first sound of the abbreviation is a vowel or a consonant.

The Full Explanation

Let's start by sorting out the difference between acronyms and initialisms.

An acronym is an abbreviation, the initial components of which can be put together and pronounced as a word or phrase. For example:

LASER
    Light
    Amplification by
    Stimulated
    Emission of
    Radiation

While still technically an acronym, *laser* has pretty much become accepted as a word, so it no longer has to be entirely capitalized. A few other examples of acronyms:

NATO

ROM and RAM

SCUBA (which is now also accepted as a word, and can be written *scuba*)

GUI (pronounced like *gooey*)

Some acronyms take the first few letters of the component words rather than just the first letter of each word. For example:

Benelux – Belgium, the Netherlands, and Luxembourg

Interpol – International Criminal Police Organization

An initialism is an abbreviation that is spoken by pronouncing each letter in it. For example:

FBI

CIA

DOA

MIA

IRS

POV (point of view or, if you're military, privately owned vehicle)

EOD (end of day; if you're military, you probably say COB [close of business] instead)

A few exceptions exist, which can be pronounced either as words, or by speaking each letter. One such example is ASAP. Another is URL, which some people do pronounce as "earl," but which I think sounds a little odd. Up to you.

Put it Into Practice

Whether an acronym or initialism takes *a* or *an* depends on the first letter or sound of the abbreviation. For example:

Several world leaders attended a NATO summit in Madrid.

The correct article is *a* because you're pronouncing NATO as a word rather than pronouncing the *N* as a letter. When in doubt, say it out loud:

Several world leaders attended an NATO summit in Madrid.

When you try to say this out loud, you should hear either the article and the acronym running together, or an awkward stop between *an* and the *N* sound.

The same is true for initialisms.

> Unfortunately, Jake found himself the subject of an IRS audit.

The correct article is *an* because you're pronouncing the letter *I* the same way you do when you're spelling a word. If you're ever in doubt, say it out loud:

> Unfortunately, Jake found himself the subject of a IRS audit.

When you say that sentence aloud, you should hear the awkward "uh aye" stumbling block.

8. There is a Better Way to Write

Some things are perfectly acceptable in spoken conversation. But when used in writing, they tend to stand out, and can even weaken your prose.

A few examples of this are *there is, there are, there was,* and *there were,* as well as *here is* and *here are.*

The Short Reason

These are obvious and—let's be honest—boring ways to state, well, anything. You can say the same thing with more dynamic vocabulary and structure.

The Full Explanation

The short reason pretty much covers it. Let's get into the examples.

Put it Into Practice

To tell the reader about the existence or location of something, you may write something like:

> There was a large table in the room.

This is kind of boring, don't you think? This is where we get into a bit of advice writers hear quite often—**show, don't tell**. Rather than simply telling the reader there was a large table, and it was in the room, you could show the table's size, color, its location and even its purpose with a bit of rearranging and additional words:

The mahogany table took up most of the dining room.

Your reader now has an idea of the table's color (and the type of wood it's made from), what the table is used for, and what room it's in. And your reader also knows it's a pretty big table if it's taking up most of the space in a room.

Let's look at another example:

Here are some editing tips to use for your next book.

Now, if you bought this book, you already know what it's about from reading the title. You know this book contains editing tips, and you know they're aimed at books because the title also says this book is for indie authors (although most of these editing tips could be used for almost any kind of writing). So why would I begin this section with that sentence? This is essentially a simplistic restating of this book's title, and it's unnecessary.

9. Prepositions and Their Pronouns

Out of all the parts of speech (and you'll see debate about exactly how many exist), prepositions are my favorite. Their essential function is to describe an object's or person's location or relationship to other objects or people. They allow us to do so many things! We can be in, out, about, before and after so many places and situations, all thanks to prepositions.

In order to accurately describe those relationships with prepositions, we need to use the right pronouns.

The Short Reason

Simply put, prepositions require certain pronouns.

The Full Explanation

Most often, prepositions take the objective form of a pronoun rather than the subjective form.

Subjective forms are *I, we, he, she,* and *you.* This means those pronouns can act as the subject of a sentence, and perform action.

Objective forms are *me, us, him, her,* and *you* again. They can be either direct or indirect objects of a sentence, and receive action.

When you use a pronoun with a preposition, that pronoun becomes an object of the preposition, which is why you must use the objective form.

Put it Into Practice

The most common pronoun abuse I see is with the preposition *between*:

> Between you and I, pronoun abuse like this drives me nuts!

I think a lot of people use *I* in this way because they feel it sounds more proper. However, it's incorrect. The correct structure is:

> Between you and me, I much prefer to be correct than sound proper.

Once you understand which pronoun forms to use with prepositions, it should be pretty easy to remember. But if this one in particular gives you some trouble, think about other prepositional object structures:

> The magazine article about him said he was born in California.

Would you say:

> The magazine article about he said he was born in California?

Of course you wouldn't. In this sentence, *about* is the preposition, so the pronoun referring to the person the magazine article is about must be an objective pronoun— *him*.

Let's look at a few more examples:

The man in line before him ordered a double espresso.

Sarah looked up and saw a chandelier above her.

The ghostly shape moved toward me.

Adam is going to the movie with us.

In these sentences, the prepositions are *before, above, toward,* and *with,* so they take the objective pronouns *him, her, me,* and *us.*

Try replacing the objective pronouns with their subjective forms (*he, she, I,* and *we*), and you'll see how silly they sound. Then you'll also see how silly *between you and I* sounds.

This same rule applies when you have more than one person in the sentence:

The man in line before Carol and him ordered a double espresso.

Sarah, Joe and I looked up and saw a chandelier above us.

The ghostly shape moved toward Greg and me.

If you're ever in doubt, remove the other person or people from the sentence to know which pronoun to use. For example, if you say:

The ghostly shape moved toward Greg and I.

And then you remove Greg, you're left with:

The ghostly shape moved toward I.

You know it should be:

The ghostly shape moved toward me.

It doesn't matter how many other people are in that haunted house with you, *me* is the correct pronoun.

And to reiterate one more time, it's always *between you and me*, never *between you and I*.

10. Prepositional Phrases and Subject-Verb Agreement

Oh, the mayhem prepositional phrases can cause! If you're not careful, those little troublemakers can wreak all kinds of havoc with your sentence structure.

When you use prepositional phrases, you must be careful not to let them lead you to use the wrong verb forms.

The Short Reason

A prepositional phrase is seldom the subject of a sentence, and instead acts as a modifier for the actual subject. Therefore, the verb must agree with the subject—not with the prepositional phrase.

The Full Explanation

It's basically subject-verb agreement, but it'll be easier to explain this particular trap through examples.

Put it Into Practice

You know basic sentence structure requires a subject and a predicate, and if the predicate contains a verb, it's usually being performed by the subject:

Craig reads science fiction novels and stories.

The subject is *Craig*, and he's performing the action *reads*. But what if Craig were reading from a recommended list?

> The list of science fiction novels were all the ones Craig wanted to read.

Of course, we know Craig wants to read novels, not the list. But *list* is the subject of the sentence. The prepositional phrase *of science fiction novels* describes the list. The verb must agree with the subject *list* rather than with the object of the preposition, *novels*. Which means the sentence should be:

> The list of science fiction novels was all the ones Craig wanted to read.

Yuck! That sounds weird now, doesn't it? We've created a huge stumbling block by putting a plural noun (*novels*) right next to a singular verb form (*was*).

To fix it, not only do we need to ensure correct subject-verb agreement, it'll be best if we change a few words, or even rearrange the sentence completely:

> The list of science fiction novels contained all the ones Craig wanted to read.

This is slightly better, but still awkward. How about:

> Craig wanted to read all the science fiction novels on the list.

Much better.

As much as I love prepositions, I actively try to avoid using prepositional phrases in this way specifically to avoid this kind of confusing structure. Make it easier on yourself—and your readers—by opting for simpler, more straightforward structures.

We're not done with prepositions yet! Read on to find out how these little tricksters can mess with your modifiers.

11. Prepositional Phrases and Misplaced Modifiers

Like real estate, getting prepositional phrases right is often about location, location, location. Where in your sentence you place your prepositional phrase can mean the difference between a well-constructed sentence and an awkward, possibly hilarious misplaced modifier mess.

The Short Reason

If you put your prepositional phrase in the wrong place, it can change the meaning of your sentence, and be distracting to the reader as they try to figure out what you really meant.

The Full Explanation

This one is easiest to illustrate and explain with examples.

Put it Into Practice

How many times have you seen blog post and article headlines like this:

> The 30 Most Popular Digital Cameras with our Readers

Are the cameras located with the readers? Of course not. But that's what the prepositional phrase *with our readers* makes it sound like because it immediately follows *cameras*. Let's try rearranging this:

> The 30 Digital Cameras Most Popular with our Readers

Much better. Here's another one:

> The kids camped out in the back yard with a thermos full of milk and cookies.

Now, we know the kids have milk, and they have cookies, but the cookies aren't also stored in the thermos along with the milk. Or maybe they are, and the kids are spooning that concoction out of the thermos, which actually sounds kind of yummy. But for this tip's illustration purposes, let's stick with the milk and cookies being separate. Again, it comes down to rearranging and adding a few more explanatory words:

> The kids camped out in the back yard with a box of cookies and a thermos full of milk.

Although these messy constructions can be deciphered with a little common sense, they're stumbling blocks and are best avoided.

12. Avoid Adverbs

I'm not going to say you should never use adverbs, but they should definitely be used sparingly. At worst, they can look like fluff or an attempt by the author to micromanage the details of a scene rather than leaving them to the reader's imagination.

At best…no, there's really no *at best* here.

The Short Reason

Because in his book, *On Writing*, Stephen King said so. OK, seriously, it's because in most cases, they're unnecessary. But still, if Stephen King says you should be doing a certain thing with your writing, it's probably in your best interest to listen to him. Who knows what might happen to you if you don't?

The Full Explanation

The short reason pretty much covers it. Adverbs, in most cases, don't really add much to your prose. In fact, they can detract from it.

Put it Into Practice

Adverbs can sometimes be lazy ways to describe things that would be better described with better adjectives. One of the worst offenders is "very." For example:

When Jerry walked into the room and saw his girlfriend kissing Steve, he was very angry.

If your character was angry, do you really need to say he was "very angry"? Does the degree of his anger matter? If it does, try using a word other than *angry*. For example:

When Jerry walked into the room and saw his girlfriend kissing Steve, he was livid.

Or maybe he was furious, or enraged. Any one of those is much more illustrative than the boring "very angry."

Make friends with your thesaurus. Look for that ideal adjective to convey the emotions or conditions you're writing about rather than adding "very" to a basic adjective. But don't go overboard with it, which we're going to discuss in the next section.

13. Pack up Your Adjectives

While usually not as extraneous as adverbs tend to be, adjectives can still bog down your work in a couple of ways. You can either describe something so meticulously that it leaves nothing to the readers' imaginations, or you can get lazy and depend too much on basic adjectives to do your work for you.

The Short Reason

Here's where we talk about one of the most commonly given pieces of writing advice:

Show, don't tell.

The Full Explanation

Whether you're writing fiction, poetry, or a white paper, you want the reader to stay engaged. You want them to enjoy what they're reading. And you want them to read to the end. Don't take the *telling* in *storytelling* literally.

Tell your story, but in such a way that it activates your readers' imaginations, gets them thinking about solutions, or evokes emotion because they relate to a character or a situation.

Put it Into Practice

Let's refer back to the previous example:

> When Jerry walked into the room and saw his girlfriend
> kissing Steve, he was livid.

Instead of telling the reader what Jerry was feeling, show
them:

> When Jerry walked into the room and saw his girlfriend
> kissing Steve, his stomach lurched, and he could feel his
> pulse pounding in his head. He picked up a brass
> statuette from the bookcase, and hurled it at his best
> friend's head. It glanced off Steve's forehead, splitting
> the skin, and sending a stream of blood into his eye.

Do you think Jerry's angry in that scene?

The other thing this does is propel the story forward. To
simply say Jerry was angry, or even that Jerry was livid,
brings the action to a halt, making a little more work for you
to get it going again, and potentially losing your readers'
interest while you do that.

In the illustrative example, the action never stops, and now
your readers are waiting to see what happens next. Will Jerry
and Steve get into a fight? Maybe Jerry's going to kill Steve.
Or maybe Steve will die later from a brain hemorrhage, and

Jerry will find himself in jail. And what's the cheating girlfriend going to do?

In non-fiction books, or business writing such as case studies or white papers, you may not write any exciting scenes about infidelity and assault with a deadly knickknack, but you can still make the writing interesting.

For example, if you're discussing statistics, rather than simply stating them, or explaining what is obvious in a graph or chart, talk about the effects of that data instead:

> As you can see in this colorful graph, sales this year were up 12% over last year.

Well, if they can see it in the graph, why would you tell them what they're looking at? And do you really need to tell them the graph is colorful? It's unlikely you're using a monochrome graph, which would kind of defeat its purpose. Try this:

> The 12% increase in sales translates to an 8% increase in company valuation, as well as a two-point bump in the stock price.

You're referring to the data in the graph but you're also providing more information, and a different context of what that data means and why it's important. (By the way, I'm making those numbers up. Please don't look to me for investing advice. Dammit, Jim, I'm a writer, not a financial advisor!)

So while "show, don't tell" may be a platitude, it's still one of the most effective tactics you can use in your writing.

14. Subjugate the Subjunctive

English can get very specific with verb forms and the appropriate times to use them. The subjunctive mood is a perfect example, and the most common predicament is when to use *was* vs. *were*.

The Short Reason

When you're expressing a wish, or discussing a conditional situation, you must use a subjunctive verb.

The Full Explanation

Every verb has a subjunctive form. For simplicity's sake, let's focus on the verb *to be*, and its forms *was* (past tense) and *were* (subjunctive mood). When you use *was*, it's to express something that has actually happened. When you want to express something that has not happened, or may never happen, use *were*.

Except! You knew there was going to be an exception, right? It's not English without an exception to the rule.

You might use *was* for something that hasn't happened yet if it's something that happens on a regular basis, or is likely to happen.

We're gonna need a bigger boat. Or maybe just some examples.

Put it Into Practice

If you're wishing for something that's unlikely to come true, or putting conditions on actions, use the subjunctive *were*, most often with *if*:

> If I were taller, I'd be able to reach the top shelf in my closet.

> If you were to win the lottery, you could buy a private island.

These are both examples of wishful thinking, and being able to reach the shelf and buy the island are conditional upon those wishes coming true.

Now let's say Amanda visits the library every week to check out the latest bestseller. The librarian might say:

> If Amanda was to come in this afternoon, she could check out Sue Grafton's latest.

Because Amanda comes in every week, and it's likely she's also going to come in this week, the librarian uses *was* instead of *were*.

Now let's say Amanda moves to another city. In this case, the librarian might say:

If Amanda were to come in today, I'd hug her because I've missed her.

Although Amanda used to visit the library every day, she no longer will because she lives too far away, so it's wishful thinking on the librarian's part. Hence, the subjunctive.

Note: The subjunctive mood is one of the more complex areas in English grammar. I've barely scratched the surface here just to offer a small push in the right direction. I highly recommend a bit more homework in order to really get a good handle on it. The other option is to do what many writers do—avoid using the subjunctive at all to save yourself the hassle. But where's the fun in that?!

15. Good, Better, Best

While you don't want to go overboard with adjectives and adverbs in your writing, when you *do* use them, make sure it's in the best, most efficient way possible.

The Short Reason

Some adjectives and adverbs can transform for comparisons, while others require the addition of *more* or *most* to do so.

The Full Explanation

Adjectives and adverbs have three forms to illustrate degrees of comparison—positive, comparative, and superlative. For example:

Positive: strong

Comparative: stronger

Superlative: strongest

Some adjectives and adverbs are irregular, in that their forms change drastically, sometimes not even resembling each other:

Positive: good, bad

Comparative: better, worse

Superlative: best, worst

Still others don't change at all, and you must add *more* and *most* to create the comparative and superlative comparisons:

Positive: likely, common

Comparative: more likely, more common

Superlative: most likely, most common

Put it Into Practice

The full explanation pretty much covers it. But sometimes, it's not a matter of being unaware of comparative and superlative forms, but of poor word order. For example:

Steel is more rigid and strong than plastic.

If you take out *rigid and*, you have *more strong*, which is incorrect because *strong* has a comparative form in *stronger*.

But if you use *stronger* in the above sentence, you'll have *more stronger*, which is even worse than what you started with. The answer is to rearrange the sentence to avoid that awkwardness:

Steel is stronger and more rigid than plastic.

16. Complicated Comparatives

I don't know about you, but this one has tripped me up for years. *Years*, I tell you. Do you do something more than *she*, or more than *her*? Pronouns can be your buddy most of the time, but when it comes to comparative adjectives, you may as well throw out your preconceived notions right now. It's about to get tricky in here, but perhaps also liberating.

The Short Reason

Comparatives were created to make us crazy. That's the short reason. OK, not really, but it *feels* that way. Long story short, you can use *as/than she* or *as/than her*, and both will be correct. You may want to jump to the full explanation for this one.

The Full Explanation

Comparative adjectives compare two things, and are structured using either *as* or *than*, depending on whether those two things are similar to, or different from each other.

To get this one down, you need to first understand how comparative adjectives are formed, and decide whether *than* is a conjunction or a preposition.

The comparative form of an adjective depends on how many syllables it has. An adjective that either has one syllable or ends in *y* takes an *er* ending to form a comparative. For example:

strong – stronger

tall – taller

bold – bolder

Some adjectives don't have comparative forms, and must be paired with *more* in order to be used in comparisons:

fun – more fun

beautiful – more beautiful

careful – more careful

Put it Into Practice

When comparing two things that are the same, the adjective will not change, and you'll use *as [adjective] as* to make the comparison. For example:

James is as strong as Ben.

Debbie is as tall as Gail.

French Roast coffee is as bold as Colombian coffee. (Debatable, but work with me.)

Swimming is as fun as running.

You can use a similar structure when comparing two things that are not the same, simply by adding *not* to the *as [adjective] as* structure:

James is not as strong as Ben.

Debbie is not as tall as Gail.

French Roast coffee is not as bold as Colombian coffee.

Swimming is not as fun as running.

Another way to compare two things that are not the same, rather than using the *not as [adjective] as* structure, is to shorten the comparison by using the comparative form of the adjective, and adding *than* to the structure.

So then you have:

Ben is stronger than James.

Gail is taller than Debbie.

Colombian coffee is bolder than French Roast coffee.

Swimming is more fun than running.

Here's the tricky part. How do you form this structure with pronouns? Specifically, pronouns that refer to people, not things. Is it:

Ben is stronger than him.

Gail is taller than her.

Or, is it:

Ben is stronger than he.

Gail is taller than she.

The confusion occurs because in the second examples, a second complete sentence is implied, which would make *than* a conjunction, whose function is to connect two complete sentences to create one sentence:

Ben is stronger [first sentence] than [conjunction] he is [second complete sentence].

Gail is taller [first sentence] than [conjunction] she is [second complete sentence].

However—and this is the really important part—**both are correct**. Well, both can be correct. You'll still find those who like to debate the topic on the basis of whether *than*, in this structure, is a preposition (which would take *him* or *her*), or a conjunction (which would require *he* or *she*).

The general consensus, though, is that using *he* or *she* in comparative structures sounds more formal, which is why most people prefer *him* or *her*.

If you're a stickler, or you think the *him/her* option may be a stumbling block for your readers, simply add the implied second clause at the end to satisfy everyone. Depending on what you're saying, though, that could potentially make for some very long and repetitive sentences. Whichever path you choose, remember to be consistent.

But wait, there's more! What about this sentence?

Jaime likes Howard more than me.

Jaime likes Howard more than I.

With this particular verb, the pronoun you choose can change the meaning of the sentence. Which pronoun you choose will depend on what you're trying to say:

Jaime likes Howard more than [she likes] me.

Jaime likes Howard more than I [do].

Again, it's probably best to add the implied portion of the clause to be clear.

17. Apostrophes

Amazing how one little punctuation mark can do so many things—and cause so much trouble. The apostrophe is probably one of the most misused and abused punctuation marks in English. Once you understand its true functions, though, it should be easy to use them well.

The Short Reason

Apostrophes are used to form contractions, indicating an omitted letter or letters. They're also used to show possession for nouns, but not for pronouns. Finally, they should seldom be used to make nouns plural. There are, of course, exceptions.

The Full Explanation

Pretty much the same as the short reason. We're going to need several examples for this one.

Put it Into Practice

Contractions

Contractions are important in several types of writing because they convey a casual tone. They're also essential to dialogue. Unless your characters are 24th century androids incapable of forming them, you'll want to include contractions so they sound more natural, and closer to the way most of us speak every day.

To illustrate how contractions are formed:

> *Don't* is a combination of *do* and *not*. The letter O in *not* is omitted, so an apostrophe takes its place.

Other similar contractions include:

> isn't — is not
>
> it's — it is (not to be confused or interchanged with *its*, which shows possession)
>
> didn't — did not
>
> there's — there is
>
> we'll — we will
>
> you're — you are
>
> I've — I have
>
> I'd've – I would have (this is a double contraction)
>
> wouldn't've – would not have (also a double contraction)
>
> would've — would have
>
> could've — could have

must've — must have

Note: I've often seen people write those last three examples as *would of, could of,* and *must of.* This stems from writing them the way they sound when spoken aloud, but is incorrect.

Sometimes one contraction can replace two different word combinations. For example:

you'd can either mean *you would* or *you had*

In this instance, *had* is more often the past participle rather than simply past tense, as in:

"If you'd taken computer classes in high school, you could've been a programmer."

Had can also be used as more of an expression when giving advice, by using *had better* plus an infinitive verb without its precedent *to*:

"You'd better get to class on time."

"You'd better not tell Mom I skipped school today."

"You'd better believe it!"

Possession
Showing possession is usually pretty easy, with a couple of tricky exceptions. For most nouns, it's a simple matter of

adding *'s* (singular possessive) or *s'* (plural possessive) to indicate when something belongs to someone or something:

Judy's purse was stolen from the locker room.

The gym's pool was too crowded for me to swim laps.

Most customers' experiences with the personal trainers were good.

The workout rooms' windows created a bright, energetic atmosphere.

Certain pronouns already indicate possession, and never need apostrophes:

This book is his.

That office is hers.

The bird lost a few of its feathers in the wind.

As mentioned previously, *it's* is never to be used as a possessive pronoun. If it were, you'd have:

The bird lost a few of it is feathers in the wind.

If you're ever in doubt, break out the contraction to see whether it works, and you'll know whether to use the apostrophe or not.

Plural Nouns

Nouns become plural by adding *s* or *es* to the end of the word, if they don't change form altogether (*mouse* to *mice*, for example). Apostrophes should never be used to indicate plurals.

house — houses **not** house's

couch — couches **not** couch's

Initialisms and Numerals

The tendency to use apostrophes to pluralize initialisms is understandable since both have several letters omitted. But initialisms, as well as numerals, become plural most often by simply adding a lowercase *s*:

TV — TVs

ABC — ABCs

GED — GEDs

30s (when referring to age)

'30s (when referring to the calendar decade; the apostrophe stands in for the omitted 19)

Note: Oxford Dictionaries says it's acceptable to write 30's. The Chicago Manual of Style says it's not. Here's the thing: If you're making plurals out of initialisms without the apostrophe, then leaving it off numerals will create consistency, and avoid confusing your readers. Whichever authority you decide to follow, be consistent in your writing.

Letters

And here's the exception for using apostrophes to make a noun plural: Letters. For example:

Mind your P's and Q's.

Some publications prefer to pluralize letters without the apostrophe, but look what happens here:

Be sure to dot your i's and cross your t's.

Without that apostrophe, you're dotting your *is*. Same goes for the letters A and U. All three of those letters become words with the addition of an S.

The apostrophe is necessary to indicate pluralization so you're not just spelling out *is*, *as*, and *us*. And because the apostrophe is necessary for those three letters, you'll want to use it on all plural letters for consistency's sake.

Shortened Words

Some words are simply shorter versions of the full word. These also simply take an *s* (or possibly *es*) to become plural, and may be altered a bit to form the new, shortened word:

professionals — pros

abdominal muscles — abs

independent authors (artists, musicians, etc.) — indies

18. Quotation Marks

Much like the apostrophe, quotation marks get quite a workout, and not always in the best way. In most cases, it's just "bad" usage.

The Short Reason

Quotation marks, also called simply quotes, have several jobs. They can indicate dialogue or, as their name suggests, quotes attributed to an actual speaker. They can also be used to illustrate definitions, or to indicate a word being used in a way that suggests something other than that word's actual definition.

The Full Explanation

The short reason covers how quotes are used. To get into more detail, let's look at some examples.

Put it Into Practice

Quotes

When quoting something a person has said, it's necessary to use quotes to let the reader know they're not your original words. Quotation marks indicate attribution so the person who spoke the words you're sharing receives proper credit. I'll use one of my favorite quotes from Eleanor Roosevelt as an example:

"You gain strength, courage and confidence by every experience in which you really stop to look fear in the face. You are able to say to yourself, 'I have lived through this horror. I can take the next thing that comes along.' You must do the thing you think you cannot do."

Make note of those single quotation marks within her quote. We'll get to those in a minute.

Dialogue

If you're writing fiction, your characters will need to speak to help move the story along. You'll indicate this with quotation marks:

Amy narrowed her eyes and said, "If you're going to pull a gun on me, you'd better be ready to use it."

"Oh, I am," Marlena said, drawing back the hammer. "I'm just trying to decide where to put the bullet."

Definitions

You can use quotes when defining a term, or when explaining a concept that may be unfamiliar to your readers:

Buying and selling stock based on privileged information is known as "insider trading."

Placing keywords strategically on a Web page is just one tactic within a larger strategy known as "search engine optimization."

Contrasted Meanings

When you use a word that has one clear definition, but you mean the opposite, you can show this by putting the word in quotes. The most common way to use this is when conveying sarcasm:

My "friend" the cop just wrote me a speeding ticket.

When to Use Single Quotation Marks

If you're quoting someone within dialogue, indicate the secondary quote with single quotation marks:

"I saw the victim running down the alley, yelling, 'Don't shoot me!' just before I heard the gunshot."

You'll notice the punctuation (in this case, an exclamation point) on that secondary quote falls inside the single quotation mark.

When Punctuation Falls Outside Quotation Marks

Ah, here's where it can get a little tricky. I think one of the best ways to illustrate this is with a title of a movie or book:

Have you seen the movie "Chef"?

My favorite book by Stephen King is "The Stand"!

Because in those cases, neither the question mark nor the exclamation point are part of those titles, they must be placed outside the quotation marks.

Note: Depending on the medium, book and movie titles may be italicized instead of appearing inside quotation marks.

In addition, you can use quotes to set off a word you're referring to within a sentence. In those cases, the punctuation will also fall outside the quotation marks:

> How do you spell "mozzarella"?

And finally, it's most often periods, commas, question marks, and exclamation points that appear inside quotation marks. Colons, semi-colons, and dashes go outside:

> Mike recited the opening line from "Moby Dick": "Call me Ishmael."

> Teresa's favorite book was "Jane Eyre"; she practically had it memorized.

> Stephanie's favorite movie is "Blade Runner"—the original version, not the director's cut.

19. Those Pesky Homophones

Time to break out a little Greek! Homophone literally means "same sound." Now, why should we cover words that sound alike, but don't look exactly alike since we're talking about writing here? Because your brain can still trip you up along the ~~weigh~~ way.

The Short Reason

Although you may be well aware of the differences in homophone definitions, they can still sneak into your writing from time to time—I know it happens to me. It's worth making a little extra effort to look for homophone errors when editing.

The Full Explanation

Our brains play all kinds of little tricks on us. While *there*, *they're* and *their* look very different when you see them written out, because they sound exactly alike, it's possible that when you're speeding along in your writing, your brain may send the wrong one down to your fingers, and you won't even realize it.

If you're anything like me, you actually hear the words in your head as you read and write. (It's not just me, right? Right?!) So while you may very well mean to type *there*, it may come out *their*, and you won't realize it in that moment.

To make matters worse, it's not something spell check will pick up.

That said, I do see quite a few people confuse certain homophones such as *your* and *you're*, so let's take a quick look at which ones go where.

Put it Into Practice

Let's take a look at some homophones often confused in writing.

There — location:

I've never been to Disney World. Have you ever been there?

Their — third person plural possessive adjective:

Jim and Jane live here. It's their apartment.

They're — contraction of *they are*:

Have you seen the Harry Potter movies? They're awesome!

Your — second person possessive adjective:

Does this book belong to you? Then it's your book.

You're — contraction of *you are*:

If you don't hurry, you're going to miss the party.

Its — neutral singular possessive adjective:

The dog lay on its back and waited for a belly rub.

It's — contraction of it is:

It's too bad you'll miss the party because it's going to be a lot of fun!

To — preposition indicating direction, place or position; also part of infinitive verbs:

Are you going to the office to work on that proposal?

Too — an adverb indicating inclusion or an excessive amount:

I'd like to go hiking too, but I have too much work to do, and I'm too tired.

Two — a number:

I've worked at this company for two years.

20. The Overuse of Overused Words You Overuse

As a writer, you probably have a certain word or phrase you like. A lot. Maybe you even love that word or phrase. It becomes a problem when you love that word or phrase so much, you use that word or phrase too much. And it really becomes a problem when you use that word or phrase so much, the reader gets sick of the word or phrase, and instead of simply reading your book, makes a game out of counting how many times you've used that word or phrase.

See what I mean?

The problem becomes serious when that reader then takes to the Internet to leave a diatribe about how you hit them over the head so many times with that favorite of yours.

The Short Reason

It's distracting, and can be seen as either pedantic or just plain lazy.

The Full Explanation

I say it's distracting because, as I already mentioned, when you write something over and over and over again, it really starts to stand out to the reader, and you run the risk of it eclipsing the rest of your text.

Depending on the word you insist on repeating, you may come off as pedantic. Are you choosing a less-commonly-used, more complex word when a simple, everyday word will do? Are you trying to entertain your readers? Or are you taking it upon yourself to ~~alienate~~ educate them?

And finally, repeatedly opting for the same word can also be perceived as laziness. Couldn't you come up with a different word this time? Couldn't you bother breaking out the thesaurus and changing things up a little? Readers can find this aggravating. I know I do.

I read a novel several years ago in which the author continually used the word "happenstance." Although it's not as commonly used as, say, *coincidence* or *by chance*, I wouldn't have minded if he'd thrown it out there two or three times, but it started to appear several times per chapter, to the point where I became so annoyed, it was a chore to finish the book.

Put it Into Practice

I don't think it's really necessary to illustrate this one with examples (other than the first paragraph in this section). Remember to be aware of the vocabulary you're using, mix it up, and don't let your love of certain words interfere with your storytelling.

21. The Unparalleled Parallel Structure

This final tip isn't really about grammar, but about a writing tactic. It's entirely possible to write a sentence that is technically grammatically correct, yet still reads poorly, and creates a huge stumbling block. Creating sentences that are parallel in structure makes for better writing, and a better reading experience.

The Short Reason

In sentences that contain two or more similar elements, you create parallel structure by ensuring they remain in the same context.

The Full Explanation

Yup, you guessed it. This one's best illustrated with examples.

Put it Into Practice

Let's say you're listing things you're going to do at work:

> On Monday, I have to write a proposal, a report, and my assistant will be on vacation.

Huh? The sentence starts out with two things you have to do—more specifically, two things you have to write—and then suddenly shifts to say what your assistant will be doing. So the first two items are within the same context, while the third is not. This is called *faulty parallelism*.

This sentence can be fixed in several ways:

> On Monday, I have to write a proposal and a report, and my assistant will be on vacation.

This is slightly better. By adding *and* before *a report*, you've made it clear it's a second thing you have to write. It puts *report* in context with *proposal*, but the part about the assistant, while grammatically correct, is still not part of the parallel structure. Why would you be mentioning the assistant? Here's one way to relate all those things:

> On Monday, I have to write a proposal and a report, both without the help of my assistant, who will be on vacation.

It works, and it makes sense, but it's a little clunky. Adding the extra bit of explanation does put the assistant being on vacation in the same context as the work you have to do, though. Another option is:

> On Monday, I have to write a proposal, a report, and an employee evaluation.

Bingo! Parallel structure achieved! All three items remain in the same context. They're all things you have to do, all things you have to write. Your tasks wouldn't all necessarily have to be things you have to write, though:

> On Monday, I have to write a proposal, attend a client meeting, and interview a new assistant.

Again, all three tasks are in the same context—the sentence maintains parallel structure.

You made it through all 21 tips! Let's move on to self-editing and how best to go about it.

PART THREE

SELF-EDITING

How to Self-Edit

Now that you know some things to look for, let's talk about how to put these tips into action and actually edit your work.

Let me start by saying some of these self-editing suggestions are based on my own experience and preferences while a couple are simply based on knowledge of alternative methods. Some of these tactics may not work for you, or you may not agree with one or two of them. That's fine. Try out the ones that appeal to you, combine them, mix and match, but most importantly, find the method that works best for *you.*

Avoid Multitasking

Don't edit while you're writing. Yes, you may catch a typo while you're writing, hit the backspace, correct it, and move on. That's probably a habit by now. I know it is for me. But save the in-depth editing for when you're actually done writing. Whether that means upon completion of a section, chapter, or the entire book is up to you.

When you're writing, just write. Get your ideas out. Get the words down. Complete your thoughts without the distractions of punctuation problems and grammar gaffes. You can always edit later, but that really great bit of dialogue you came up with for your heroine may evaporate if you allow yourself to get caught up in the editing.

Take a Break

Once you're done writing and are ready to move into the editing phase, close your document and walk away for a little while. Take a break and allow your mind to get a little bit of distance from your work. Whether it's an hour, a day, or a week is up to you. A break will give you broader perspective, and make you better able to see those little errors you may not notice if you write your last word and immediately begin editing what you just wrote.

Use Find and Replace

One of the best word processing inventions (aside from Undo, and Copy and Paste) is Find and Replace. Use it to search for instances of *that* to determine which ones can stay and which should go. If Oxford commas are a concern for you, search punctuation to make sure you've been consistent. Do you prefer *more than* to *over*? Find and replace. It's an editor's best friend.

Read Out Loud

Sometimes, the best way to find and fix errors and stumbling blocks is to read your work out loud. Actually speaking the words you've written will help you identify where the natural pauses should be, and can make things like misplaced modifiers really stand out.

Read Backwards

Sounds weird, right? But think about it. You've taken a lot of time writing your book. You've lived with it for days, weeks, possibly months, or even longer. You know every plot twist, every character idiosyncrasy, every nook and cranny of your story. Reading it backwards will force you to really examine each word, sentence, paragraph, and page. It's like arranging furniture in a room, and then looking at it from the second floor landing—it gives you a totally different perspective so you can see where the flow may be obstructed, or how something can be rearranged to sound better.

Change Your Font

Whatever favorite font you write in (mine's Calibri), your brain gets used to it, which can make it easier for you to miss small errors. Before you edit your work, change your font to something unlike the one you normally use. For example, go from a sans serif font to a serif font. I don't recommend trying to edit in a script or other fancy font. And please, no Comic Sans. Friends don't let friends use Comic Sans. Ever.

Change Your Text Size

You can do this one alone, or in tandem with changing your font. If you normally write in 12 point, increase to 14 or even 16 for editing. Again, this will make things look different than what you've been seeing while you've been writing, and can help small errors stand out.

Check for Consistency

This is key. Once you've made a style decision (the Oxford comma, *more than* instead of *over*, etc.), set aside some of your editing time to make sure you've been consistent in that choice. If you switch back and forth between style options throughout your book, you run the risk of possibly confusing and likely annoying your readers. Find and Replace will come in handy here as well.

Take a Break

After your initial edit, take another break. Walk away, do other things, and let your manuscript sit for a little while. Again, how long of a break you take is up to you, depending on what you feel comfortable with, or whether you have a deadline.

Do it Again

Edit your manuscript again, either using the same method you implemented for the first round, or another method to increase the likelihood of finding things you may have missed the first time through.

Read Your Manuscript

The final step is to read your work from beginning to end, putting yourself in your readers' shoes. Does everything flow the way you want it to? Do you run across any confusing passages, or spots where, while editing, you mistakenly deleted an extra word, or forgot to remove one? Does the narration sound the way you want it to? How about the dialogue? Are you happy with it overall? If not, now's the time to make any final changes. If so, congratulations! You're ready to move on to the next step.

Onward to Success!

Your next step may be different from someone else's. Maybe you'll send your manuscript to another editor for one final pass in front of another set of eyes. Maybe you've enlisted the help of a few beta readers. Maybe your plan is to send out a few advance copies for early reviews. Or maybe all of the above, and more, before you actually publish.

Whatever plan you've laid out for yourself, you can rest a little easier knowing your work is stronger than it was in the first draft. You can feel confident that your beta readers and your advance reviewers will be able to provide you with more positive feedback, and better reviews.

And finally, you can publish your book knowing you've put forth your best effort, and created something to be truly proud of.

Good luck!

PART FOUR

RESOURCES

Writing and Editing Resources

I'm sharing a few of my favorite resources to use in both your editing and writing. I hope you find them helpful!

Websites

Grammar Girl – www.quickanddirtytips.com/grammar-girl

The undisputed queen of grammar, Mignon Fogarty is my first stop for grammar and punctuation questions. She explains even the most complex grammatical conundrums in a friendly and fun way.

Grammarist – grammarist.com/

This site covers grammar, spelling and even style, but you may find the Varieties of English section especially helpful if you want to convert American conventions to British (or Australian or Canadian), or vice-versa. Be sure to check out the Usage section to get the details on things like compliment vs. complement, and the dreaded "could care less."

Visual Thesaurus – www.visualthesaurus.com/

The visual representations make this a fun thesaurus to use, but what's interesting is how it can take you down a synonymous path every time you click on a word option. It also categorizes each option into parts of speech. Be aware that it's free for a limited number of searches, and then requires a subscription.

The Eggcorn Database – eggcorns.lascribe.net/

What's an eggcorn? It's an unusual, often hilarious misspelling of an English word, usually attributed to its pronunciation, and on people hearing a word and not seeing it in print. Hence, *eggcorn* rather than *acorn*. You can also contribute eggcorns you run across.

Common Errors in English Usage –
public.wsu.edu/~brians/errors/errors.html

Do you always forget the difference between *insure* and *ensure*? Do you confuse *forgo* with *forego*? Are you unsure whether to use *toward* or *towards*? If so, bookmark this site. It's been one of my favorites for years. It's also now available in independently published eBook and paperback versions, if you'd like to support another indie venture!

Purdue Online Writing Lab – owl.english.purdue.edu/owl/

This site's been around since 1995, and I use it quite often. In addition to general writing help in grammar, mechanics and punctuation, you'll find help with other areas such as academic writing, personal correspondence (great for epistolary writing), and even help with research and sourcing.

Preditors & Editors – pred-ed.com/peeslw.ht

If you do decide to hire a professional editor, but still don't feel comfortable distinguishing a good editor from a "preditor," make this site your first stop to get recommendations. It's non-profit, supported by ads and donations, so no editors are paying to have their information listed here.

Jane Friedman – janefriedman.com/

In addition to writing an excellent blog full of both traditional and self-publishing gems, Ms. Friedman teaches publishing at the University of Virginia, and offers a lot of information geared toward indie authors. I also recommend subscribing to her informative newsletter, which often contains photos of cats. Because everything's more fun with cats.

The Book Designer – www.thebookdesigner.com/

This is another fantastic blog chock-full of self-publishing advice on both the writing and business sides. Joel Friedlander also practices what he preaches, having written numerous books to help indie authors get started and navigate the self-publishing landscape.

Hugh Howey – www.hughhowey.com/

One of the most successful indie authors in the United States (if not the world), Hugh Howey writes a lot about the business of self-publishing. His posts provide invaluable insight from an insider's perspective. Plus, he seems like a nice guy, and he's pretty funny.

Books

The Elements of Style – William Strunk, Jr. and E. B. White

A classic. First published by Strunk in 1920, and then expanded and updated by White in 1959, it's widely regarded as one of the best writing reference books of all time, for good reason.

Grammar Girl's 101 Misused Words You'll Never Confuse Again – Mignon Fogarty

This book is a necessity if for no other reason than to explain the differences between *adieu* and *ado*, *affect* and *effect*, and *bad* vs. *badly*.

Grammar Girl's Punctuation 911 – Mignon Fogarty

Everything you need to know about punctuation, all in a handy quick-reference guide.

The Blue Book of Grammar and Punctuation: An Easy-to-Use Guide with Clear Rules, Real-World Examples, and Reproducible Quizzes – Jane Straus, Lester Kaufman and Tom Stern

Don't let the quiz part put you off. This is a fantastic book for getting a handle on English grammar. The examples are wonderful and very helpful to illustrate even the most complicated rules. Be aware that it does read a bit like a textbook, but the knowledge shared is worth it. You can also check out the accompanying website, www.grammarbook.com.

On Writing: A Memoir of the Craft – Stephen King

OK, so this isn't really an editing or reference book, but I'd be remiss if I didn't mention it. As learning to be a better editor will help you be a better writer, picking up some excellent writing tips will also help your editing go more smoothly. What I love about this book is King's informal voice. You can almost hear him explaining his writing philosophies to you without pretension or arrogance. He's just talking, one writer to another. I highly recommend you listen.

If you enjoyed this book...

... I'd be grateful if you'd help others find it, too. Online reviews are crucial for indie authors like me. They help bring credibility and help make books more discoverable by new readers.

If you found this book helpful, or you simply enjoyed it the way only a writer, editor, or fellow word nerd can, I would be grateful if you took a few moments to leave an honest review at one of the following websites.

Amazon.com

Goodreads.com

Thank you and thanks for reading!

Michelle

Acknowledgements

This book would not have been possible without several people to whom I am tremendously grateful. We never know what might happen tomorrow, so if I only get one shot at this, I'm making it a good one:

My mom, Rebecca Fernandez. For everything.

My friends and Rota Nation for their unending support, encouragement and love. I can't possibly list you all, but know you're in my heart.

Claire Jackson, whose own success as an indie author inspired me to take the plunge, and whose support and help made this entire process much easier and more enjoyable.

The many writers with whom I've worked over the years. Not everyone accepts edits graciously, and the ones who do stand out. Through their talent, skill, questions, and suggestions, they also helped me to become a better editor. I'm also fortunate to call some of them my friends. You know who you are.

Several members of the Writer's Café on the Kindle Boards forum who answered my newbie questions kindly, patiently, and thoroughly, and whose encouragement and generosity helped me believe this goal was well within my reach.

The animators, songwriters, singers, producers, and everyone involved in creating the *Schoolhouse Rock* series (in particular, *Grammar Rock*) that aired on Saturday mornings when I was a kid. I loved those shorts, and can still sing most of the songs. Early on, they instilled in me a love of words and grammar that continues to this day. It's because of that series that I know what a conjunction's function is. You may see a reference or two in a few of the chapters here. Bonus points to you if you spot them!

I'm grateful to every person who reads this book. A written work isn't complete until it's been read. Thank you.

Most of all, I'm grateful to and for my husband, John, who was behind me from the moment I shared with him that I wanted to write and publish a book. His support, encouragement and love never waver. I couldn't be any luckier.

I am undoubtedly leaving a few important people out. If that's you, I hope I've expressed my gratitude to you directly when I should have.

About the Author

Michelle Lowery is unaccustomed to writing about herself in the third person, but she'll give it a shot and try not to sound too pretentious, which is difficult to do when referring to oneself in the third person. And now she's thrown a *very* pretentious "one" into the mix. Let's just get to the bio stuff.

Michelle has been a professional writer and editor since 1989. Her work has appeared in numerous publications, both print and online.

She began working in the SEO and digital marketing industry in 2008, first with a few agencies, and then running her own boutique agency for two years.

She now works as a freelance copywriter and editor, with a focus on helping other indie authors, while she continues to write books.

Michelle lives in San Antonio, in her home state of Texas, with her husband and their furry and feathered kids.

If you'd like to connect with Michelle, please visit her website, **michellelowery.com**. You can also follow her on Twitter at **@MichelleDLowery**, or like her Facebook page at **facebook.com/michelleloweryauthor**.

Get a **FREE** mini-book of five more editing tips not included in this book! Just sign up for Michelle's mailing list: **michellelowery.com/mini-book/**